BP PORTRAIT AWARD 2007

National Portrait Gallery

Published in Great Britain by
National Portrait Gallery Publications,
National Portrait Gallery,
St Martin's Place, London WC2H 0HE

Published to accompany
the BP Portrait Award 2007,
held at the National Portrait Gallery, London,
from 14 June to 16 September 2007,
Laing Art Gallery, Newcastle upon Tyne,
from 13 October to 2 December 2007,
and at the Scottish National Portrait Gallery,
Edinburgh, from 14 December 2007
to 16 March 2008.

For a complete catalogue
of current publications
please write to the address above,
or visit our website at
www.npg.org.uk/publications

ISBN 978-1-85514-385-2

A catalogue record for this book
is available from the British Library.

Publishing Manager: Celia Joicey
Editor: Caroline Brooke Johnson
Design: Anne Sørensen
Production Managers:
Ruth Müller-Wirth and Tim Holton
Photography: Prudence Cuming
Travel Award photography:
Jonathan Gooding
Printed and bound in Italy

Cover: *Winter Portrait* by Ingolv Helland

PREFACE   6
Sandy Nairne

FOREWORD   7
Tony Hayward

DESCRIBING FACES   8
Lynne Truss

BP PORTRAIT AWARD 2007   16

PRIZE-WINNING PORTRAITS
Johan Andersson   18
Paul Emsley   19
David Lawton   20
Hynek Martinec   21

SELECTED PORTRAITS   22

BP TRAVEL AWARD   79

TRAVELS IN A CAMPER VAN   80
Toby Wiggins

ACKNOWLEDGEMENTS   87

INDEX   88

The purpose of the BP Portrait Award is to encourage the art of portrait painting amongst artists and to foster interest in as wide a public as possible. This idea has been central to the Gallery's interests for nearly three decades. But this year was the time for change. Up until now the competition was restricted to artists under forty and this served the particular purpose of focusing on and encouraging young talent. However, following the successes of the several generations of artists who have been prize winners and exhibitors, we have opened up the Award to everyone aged eighteen and over. In addition, a separate prize is being offered to an artist aged thirty or under.

Faced with a record entry, the jury selected from 1,870 submitted works from around the world, making choices only on the basis of the portraits as the artists' names are not declared. Every approach was evident, from the highly expressionistic, through the painterly and metaphorical, to the immaculately photo-realist in style. Some visitors in previous years have been bemused by the latter style, wondering why one medium should be used to imitate another, perhaps not recognising the amount of care and skill required to achieve the surface effect.

Whatever the debate about style, this is a painting competition in which every artist will have had direct contact with their chosen sitter. As ever, partners, friends, parents and children appear frequently as portraits of affection. They contrast with the fewer commissioned or institutional images, presented as portraits of honour.

Painted portraiture, as the BP Portrait Award so amply demonstrates, remains a vital, effective and popular form of art. This is the more so because of the increasingly digitised and media-dominated world against which it contrasts. And this exhibition gloriously celebrates this hand-crafted, painstaking and highly skilled activity.

SANDY NAIRNE
Director, National Portrait Gallery

FOREWORD

BP recognizes the importance of arts and culture for individuals, for communities and for the economy. Our UK arts and culture programme is designed to enable as many people as possible to have access to excellence in the arts. We are delighted to support some of Britain's most outstanding cultural institutions, including the National Portrait Gallery.

Our support of the BP Portrait Award was established in conjunction with the National Portrait Gallery in 1990. Since then the Award has grown in scope and stature and is now a unique and distinguished prize in the world of figurative art. The quality of the Award has been matched by a growth in the numbers who visit the exhibition each year. In 2006 there were 197,687 visitors in London alone – the highest number yet.

Following the success of the BP Portrait Award in encouraging younger artists to focus and develop the theme of painted portraiture within their work, this year we opened up the Award to a wider age range in order to enable even more artists to take part. This has led to an increase in entries of over 50 per cent this year.

BP is delighted to be associated with the BP Portrait Award. Our partnership with the National Portrait Gallery will continue at least until 2011.

I would like to thank all those who have made possible the growth and success of this very special Award over the last decade. I would also like to thank all the staff within the National Portrait Gallery who have helped establish the BP Portrait Award as an internationally recognized prize and who have helped make our partnership such a success. Principally, however, I want to acknowledge the creativity and enthusiasm of the thousands of artists whose ability to capture human character on a two-dimensional canvas is a rare and precious quality. This year, as every year, the success of the Prize is a reflection of the quality of their work.

TONY HAYWARD
Group Chief Executive, BP

One of the things that all authors of fiction must learn to judge is whether – and in what detail – to describe the face of a character. 'He remembered her slender, weak neck, her beautiful grey eyes,' writes Anton Chekhov in his 1899 short story 'Lady with a Little Dog'. 'He had thick, dark, wavy hair,' writes Raymond Chandler in *The Long Goodbye* (1953); 'He was tanned very dark. He looked up with bird-bright eyes and smiled under a hairline moustache. His tie was a dark maroon tied in a pointed bow over a sparkling white shirt.' 'Her features were dark, and still vivid with youth,' writes Sarah Waters in *The Night Watch* (2006); 'her hair was a rich brownish-black.' In *Mansfield Park* (1814), Jane Austen describes the young Fanny Price: 'She was small of her age [*sic*], with no glow of complexion, nor any other striking beauty; exceedingly timid and shy, and shrinking from notice; but her air, though awkward, was not vulgar, her voice was sweet, and when she spoke, her countenance was pretty.'

I suppose there is one obvious point to make about such facial descriptions in fiction: that they stimulate the visual imagination of the reader, but only very, very tactfully. The slender neck, the wavy hair and the dark features are offered as mere corner-of-the-eye glances, mere hints, which the reader is free to ignore: both writer and reader seem to agree that it's better to offer an impression of a bird-bright eye or a significant pallor than to attempt an exhaustive inventory of an imagined set of features. A writer has many matters to consider here, of course, most of them covered by the law of diminishing returns. Chief among these is that a character needs many things besides a face: a personal psychology, a history, a manner of speaking, a general appearance, maybe even an interesting ambulatory style – and none of these is as difficult, or as thankless, to convey in prose as the shape and detail of a set of features. How can a face ever be sufficiently described, in any case? Olivia, in Shakespeare's *Twelfth Night*, playfully rejects Viola's rehearsed flattery of her beauty by promising to give out 'schedules' of her face. '*Item*, two lips, indifferent red;

SIR JONATHAN MILLER,
b.1934
Stephen Conroy, 1999
Oil on canvas
1829 x 1219mm
(72 x 48")
National Portrait
Gallery (NPG 6492)

item, two grey eyes, with lids to them; *item*, one neck, one chin, and so forth.' Any description of any face is essentially the same as Olivia's, unless – and this doesn't happen *very* often – one of the features is actually missing.

You can see why so few authors choose to make the attempt. Listing every feature will not only fatally hold up the narrative, but may even antagonise the poor confused reader who can't remember what 'aquiline' means, and thinks that an 'almond' eye must be brown and nutty. Besides, what purpose will it serve to expend 500 words on the tilt of this particular nose and the set of this particular jaw? Does the reader require a mental identikit image of a character in order to take an interest? No, indeed. Facial detail is rarely kept in mind at all by a reader. A devotee of Charlotte Brontë's *Jane Eyre* (1847) tends to remember that, say, Mr Rochester is a dark sort of man, and that Jane is a short sort of woman, and this is quite enough to go on – especially when one's attention keeps being caught by such things as cackles from the attic and beds catching fire. It has been well noted of Gustave Flaubert's *Madame Bovary* (1857) that the colour of the heroine's eyes changes in the course of the novel – and the significant point is that a) Flaubert didn't notice, and b) generations of readers haven't noticed either.

As a writer, one can't help thinking about such matters in the rather intimidating presence of painted portraits. Take that excellent recent oil of the thoughtful, heavy-headed Jonathan Miller by Stephen Conroy (see page 9). The thing is, a well-rendered representation of a particular human being does exactly the opposite of a written description: it answers all sorts of questions about his singularity, gives us the unique face and form, but at the same time reminds us that we are all essentially – and equally – alone and unknowable. Where a writer just hints at the nose or the hair colour, a portrait just hints at all those other things about its subject: his psychology, history, manner of speaking, or (say) his idiosyncratic habit of standing on one leg and humming 'La donna è mobile' while deciding what to do. We look at portraits and we think, 'I feel I know you, Jonathan Miller, because you have been revealed to me here so perfectly', and then we think, 'But, actually, I don't know you any better at all now, do I?'

I once spent a whole year studying portraits for a literary purpose. I was writing a novel about the Tennyson circle on the Isle of Wight, and one of the many attractions of the subject was that this circle contained two great Victorian portraitists: the photographer Julia Margaret Cameron and the artist G.F. Watts. Integral to my plot, in fact, was Watts working on the National Portrait Gallery's painting called

'CHOOSING',
DAME ELLEN TERRY,
1847–1928
George Frederic Watts,
c.1864
Oil on strawboard
mounted on Gatorfoam
472 x 354mm
(18⅝ x 14")
National Portrait
Gallery (NPG 5048)

Choosing, a portrait of his young wife, Ellen Terry. As I was forming my fictional designs on the real people who populate Mrs Cameron's photographs, I felt very privileged that I could study their faces; and I was increasingly drawn to Victorian notions of physiognomy: the idea that a face is readable, and that (as Charles Dickens wrote in 1856, after seeing a murderer on trial), 'Nature never writes a bad hand. Her writing, as may be read on the human countenance, is invariably legible, if we come at all trained to the reading of it.' For the Victorians, this was the point of portraiture. Following Watts's grand injunction, 'The utmost for the highest!', Mrs Cameron was devoted to showing the inner quality of her beautiful (female) or eminent (male) sitters. She lit their eyes and temples to maximum advantage, with the result that many of her young women look like angels, and many of her old men look like God.

What now intrigues me is how far any of those old physiognomy ideas still linger in our collective mind. The 'science' of it may have been discredited long ago, yet we still judge people on facial appearance when we have nothing else to go on. Presented with the portrait of an unknown person, we analyse the features, search the expression, ask ourselves deep questions about how far we would run if we met them in a dark alley. While life experience teaches us the folly of associating (say) beauty with kindness – and we wouldn't nowadays expect to identify a murderous personality by measuring an ear lobe – yet we can still harbour indefensible prejudices about people with wonky eyes (untrustworthy) or thin lips (mean). Having learned quite a bit about phrenology (the personality as revealed by the shape, size and proportions of the skull), I tend to keep quiet about it, but I do take note when new men in my life display no visible organ of 'Amativeness' (propensity for love, found at the base of the skull), and I am willing to gamble this has saved me a lot of heartbreak further down the line.

But of course what we see in a portrait is not just a face. We see the work of an artist, whose intentions in the creation of the work are of prime importance, yet can only be inferred. How far does a portrait reflect the personality of the artist, rather than of the sitter? One of 2004's BP exhibiting artists was Darvish Fakhr, with his triptych *Three Men Named Ian* – a cheerful anti-taxonomy project in itself, of course, since it makes the useful point that the chaps have nothing in common besides their name. These are tiny pictures, each just six inches square. Each face is open and alert; thinking, but not thoughtful. The middle face beams and engages. As you look at it, you find yourself shuffling the three faces into different natural alliances, looking for common characteristics, and also marvelling at the way the artist has put so much of himself in while also keeping so much of himself out.

THREE MEN NAMED IAN,
Darvish Fakhr, 2004
Oil on board
457 x 152mm
(18 x 6")

Back with my Victorian project, while I knew the faces of my characters so well that I made scoffing can-you-believe-this noises when I found sitters misidentified in scholarly books, I still gave only minimal descriptive hints when it came to writing the novel.

I mentioned a beard here and there, or some long hair or dirty fingernails; the odd nose; some red hair clashing with a pink frock. The thing is, when a writer starts to list the specifics of a person's features, readers rightly ask themselves what's going on. Thinking about this issue, I dug out two extraordinarily detailed facial descriptions from the nineteenth century: one from Edgar Allan Poe's 1838 story 'Ligeia', the other from Anthony Trollope's 1857 novel *Barchester Towers*. In the 'Ligeia' passage ('I examined the contour of the lofty and pale forehead … . I scrutinized the formation of the chin … . The expression of the eyes of Ligeia! How for long hours have I pondered upon it!'), the overpowering detail is meant to indicate that the narrator is fixated, mad and probably quite ill as well. Meanwhile, in *Barchester Towers*'s famous and revolting description of Mr Slope ('His hair is lank, and of a dull reddish hue. It is always formed into three straight lumpy masses, each brushed with admirable precision, and cemented with much grease'), Trollope dwells on every aspect of Slope's appearance mainly to signal how much he relishes his own entitlements as the book's author.

It remains true to say, however, that discretion is the general choice for writers, for the good reason that we know when we're not wanted. There is a lovely story from the old days at *The New Yorker* about the famously demanding editor Harold Ross returning a proof to writer Robert Benchley covered in queries and marks, and Benchley sending it back to him with, 'You stay out of this, Ross' written on it. If, in a modern novel, one started to describe the arch of an eyebrow or the flare of a nostril, 'You stay out of this' would be exactly the response scribbled in the margin by the reader, annoyed to be interrupted in forming his own mental impressions. I must confess to one massive error of judgement of this kind in my own work, in my novel *Going Loco* (1999), where I couldn't resist having one character cruelly say of another, 'But Belinda looks like George Orwell!' But when I re-read the book recently, I realised that I really should have stayed out of it. Comparing a fictional character to George Orwell (especially a woman) is too big a jolt, and besides, it comes about two thirds of the way through the book. To throw into readers' minds, at such a late stage, not only a long, hawk-nosed face but a distinctive 1930s pencil moustache is simply not playing the game.

It's odd to think that the writer, whose authorship status is so plain in other ways, should face the necessity of 'staying out of it' in this area of physical description, while the viewer of a portrait is agog for any (and every) indication of the artist's hand. But the stark truth is that an invented face is an actual impossibility, while a real face, as the raw material of art, is limitless in its potential. Someone told me recently that if you cross-referenced all of Ian Fleming's hints about the appearance of James Bond, you would end up with an identikit of Sean Connery; and my impatient response was that I couldn't care less, and what a stupid waste of time. Writers and painters alike are in the business of consulting their own imaginations, and stimulating the imaginations of others. Together, and separately, they celebrate the absolute mystery of otherness.

LYNNE TRUSS
Writer and broadcaster

BP PORTRAIT AWARD 2007

The Portrait Award, in its twenty-eighth year at the National Portrait Gallery and eighteenth year of sponsorship by BP, is an annual event.

Now open to everyone over eighteen years of age, it is aimed at encouraging artists from around the world to focus upon and develop portraiture within their work. This year there is a new prize for artists aged between eighteen and thirty.

THE JUDGES

Chair: Sandy Nairne, Director, National Portrait Gallery

Jason Brooks, artist

Rachel Campbell-Johnston, Chief Art Critic, *The Times*

Sarah Howgate, Contemporary Curator,
National Portrait Gallery

Erin O'Connor, model

Des Violaris, Director, UK Arts & Culture, BP

THE PRIZES

The BP Portrait Awards are:

First Prize
£25,000, plus at the Gallery's discretion a commission worth £4,000 to paint a well-known person

Second Prize
£8,000

Third Prize
£6,000

BP Young Artist Award
£5,000

PRIZE-WINNING PORTRAITS

TAMARA
Johan Andersson
Oil on canvas, 1000 x 730mm (39³/₈ x 28³/₄")

18

MICHAEL SIMPSON
Paul Emsley
Oil on canvas, 1370 x 1120mm (53⁷/₈ x 44")

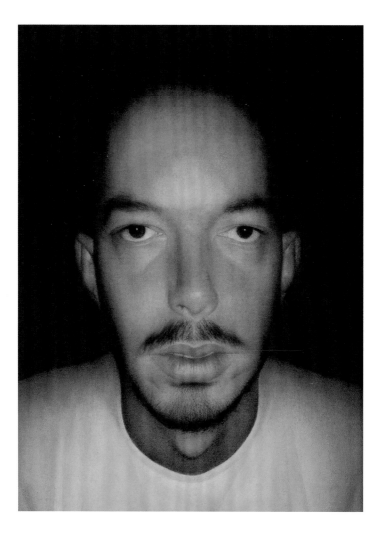

STEPHEN
David Lawton
Oil on canvas, 270 x 200mm (10⁵/₈ x 7⁷/₈")

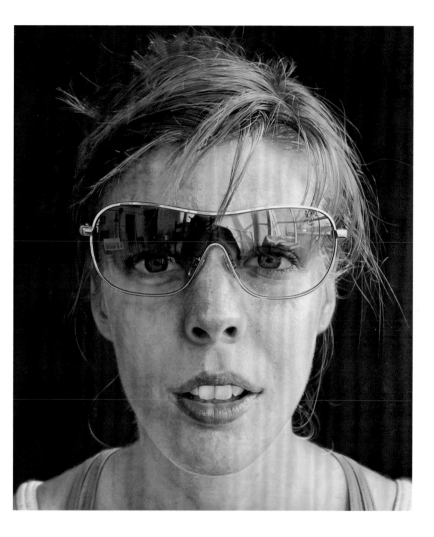

ZUZANA IN THE PARIS STUDIO
Hynek Martinec
Acrylic on canvas, 1300 x 1100mm (51¹/₈ x 43¹/₄")

SELECTED PORTRAITS

TIME TO TALK
Lynn Ahrens
Oil on canvas, 720 x 590mm (28³/₈ x 23¹/₄")

PORTRAIT OF CHRISTOPHER DARROUX-XAVIER
Rupert Alexander
Oil on canvas, 600 x 440mm (23^{5}/$_{8}$ x 17^{3}/$_{4}$")

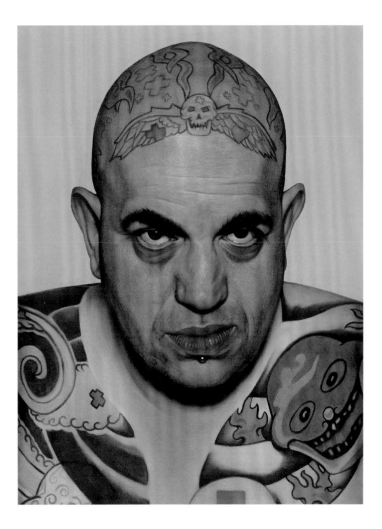

FRANKO B
Jeremy Andrews
Oil on canvas, 440 x 340mm (17³/₈ x 13³/₈")

25

MAN STARING
Maryanne Aytoun-Ellis
Egg tempera on board, 410 x 350mm (16$\frac{1}{8}$ x 13$\frac{3}{4}$")

COMMUTER
John Ball
Oil on canvas, 505 x 405mm (19$\frac{7}{8}$ x 16")

NICOLA
Polly Benford
Acrylic on board, 300 x 210mm (11$^7/_8$ x 8$^1/_4$")

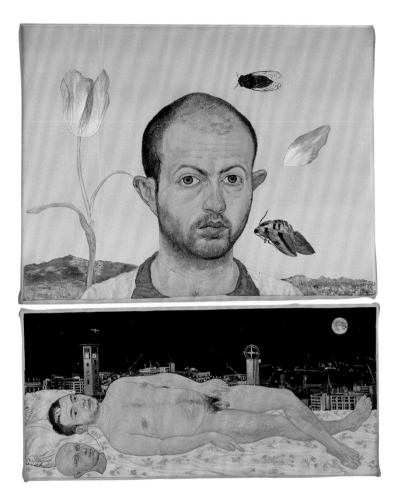

PORTRAIT
Emmanouil Bitsakis
Oil on canvas, 290 x 230mm (11³/₈ x 9")

29

JOHNNY AND GLORY
Richard Brazier
Oil on canvas, 1550 x 1190mm (61 x 46⁷/₈")

MR & MRS BROWN
Vincent Brown
Acrylic on linen, 1000 x 900mm (39³/₈ x 35¹/₂")

31

IRENE (MY WIFE)
Francis Corsham
Acrylic and water oils on hardboard, 265 x 215mm (10¹/₂ x 8¹/₂")

JOSE ESCOFET
Miriam Escofet
Oil on canvas on board, 500 x 400mm (19⅝ x 15¾")

33

NISHA
Darvish Fakhr
Oil on canvas, 2840 x 1885mm (111⁷/₈ x 74¹/₄")

34

KAVEH, AGE 31
Maryam Foroozanfar
Oil on canvas, 250 x 200mm (9⁷/₈ x 7⁷/₈")

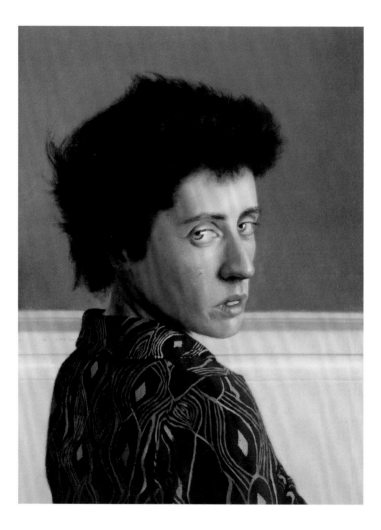

LOOKING BACK
Aram Gershuni
Oil on board, 440 x 330mm (17³/₈ x 13")

JOY
Robin-Lee Hall
Egg tempera on board, 700 x 600mm (27^1/$_2$ x 23^5/$_8$")

SELF-PORTRAIT
Jaemi Hardy
Oil on canvas on panel, 250 x 200mm (9^7/$_8$ x 7^7/$_8$")

WINTER PORTRAIT
Ingolv Helland
Oil on canvas, 545 x 395mm (21$\frac{1}{2}$ x 15$\frac{1}{2}$")

REDHEAD (SELF-PORTRAIT)
Amanda Hext
Oil on board, 400 x 400mm (15³/₄ x 15³/₄")

IAN HAMILTON FINLAY (1997–2006)
Eileen Hogan
Oil on board, triptych, each 250 x 200mm (9⁷/₈ x 7⁷/₈")

41

PUGNIS ET CALCIBUS
Jill Hooper
Oil on board, 250 x 200mm (9$^7/_8$ x 7$^7/_8$")

SHE AND ME
Timothy Hyman
Oil on board, 610 x 460mm (24 x 18$\frac{1}{8}$")

43

SELF-PORTRAIT
Kwang-Sik Im
Oil on canvas, 350 x 250mm (13³/₄ x 9⁷/₈")

THE KING OF SPAIN
Diarmuid Kelley
Oil on canvas, 1020 x 760mm (40$^{1}/_{8}$ x 29$^{7}/_{8}$")

PAINTING OF WARIS
Sandro Kopp
Oil on canvas, 535 x 725mm (21 x 28^1/$_2$")

46

A.C. GRAYLING
Thomas Leveritt
Oil on panel, 1015 x 1015mm (40 x 40")

47

FIGURA ONIRICA
Anna Madia
Acrylic on board, 405 x 495mm (15$^7/_8$ x 19$^1/_2$")

NOVELTY
Susannah Massey
Oil and acrylic on canvas, 595 x 440mm (23³/₈ x 17¹/₄")

CAMILLA
Francesco Mernini
Oil on canvas on board, 390 x 490mm (15³/₈ x 19¹/₄")

50

ALEX
Nicholas Merton
Oil on board, 460 x 320mm (18¹/₈ x 12¹/₂")

SELF-PORTRAIT
Ana Maria Micu
Oil on canvas, 500 x 500mm (19⅝ x 19⅝")

SALLY
Luis Morris
Oil on canvas, 740 x 490 (29$^1/_8$ x 19$^1/_4$")

GEORGIA IN PROFILE
Neil Nelson
Oil on canvas, 290 x 290mm (11³/₈ x 11³/₈")

54

CHUCK
Paul Oxborough
Oil on canvas, 450 x 600mm (17³/₄ x 23⁵/₈")

KATY DOES IT WHILE BAKING A CAKE
Morgan Penn
Oil on canvas, 710 x 560mm (28 x 22")

56

TIM
Scott Pohlschmidt
Oil on canvas, 385 x 285mm (15$^{1}/_{8}$ x 11$^{1}/_{4}$")

ORGANIA
Anastasia Pollard
Oil on board, 700 x 380mm (27$\frac{1}{2}$ x 15")

LOLA
Gareth Reid
Acrylic on board, 250 x 200mm (9$^7/_8$ x 7$^7/_8$")

THE BEVIN BOY
Philip Renforth
Oil on board, 545 x 330mm (21$^{1}/_{2}$ x 13")

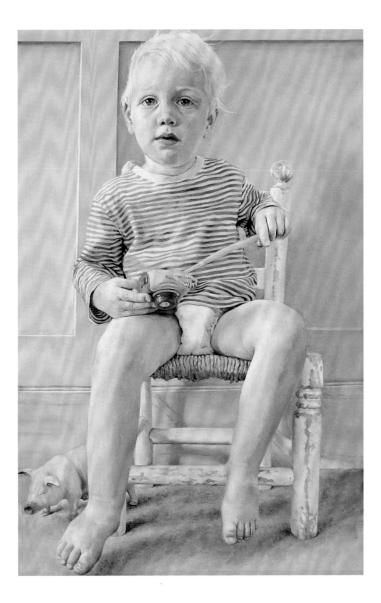

STANLEY
Keith Robinson
Oil on canvas, 750 x 490mm (29$\frac{1}{2}$ x 19$\frac{1}{4}$")

61

TOM, JAN, MIKE, CHLOE AND LILLIE – THE POTTERS
Stephen Earl Rogers
Oil on board, 780 x 1060mm (30³/₄ x 41³/₄")

RICARDO
Geert Schless
Oil on board, 1500 x 600mm (59 x 23⁵/₈")

63

AILEEN
Perdita Sinclair
Acrylic and oil on canvas, 400 x 350mm (15¾ x 13¾")

GINNIE
Benjamin Sullivan
Oil on canvas, 750 x 750mm (29½ x 29½")

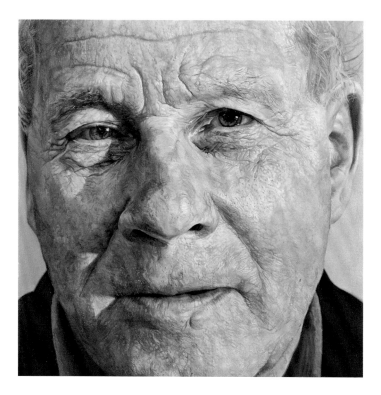

ONLY FOR A FIVER
Edward Sutcliffe
Oil on canvas, 300 x 300mm (11$^7/_8$ x 11$^7/_8$")

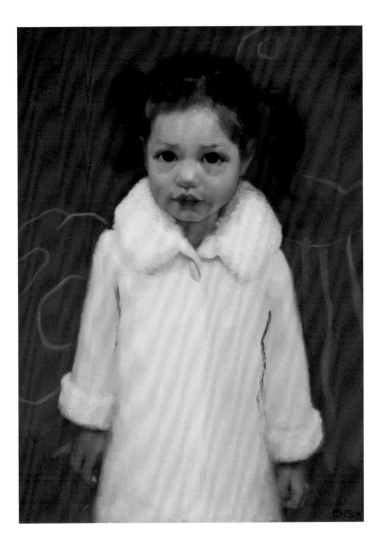

AMELIE
Cassandra Szekely
Oil on panel, 415 x 300mm (16^3/$_8$ x 11^7/$_8$")

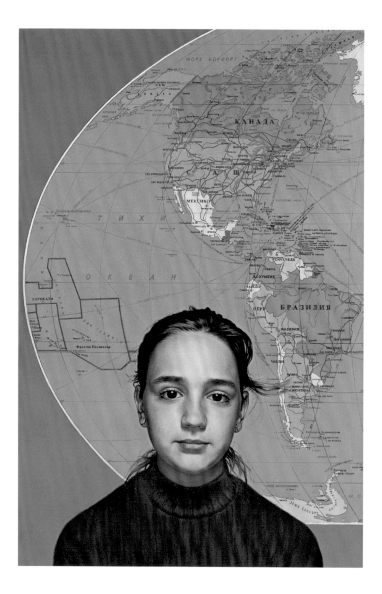

PORTRAIT OF DENITSA
Ivan Tafrov
Acrylic on canvas, 920 x 615mm (36^1/$_4$ x 24^1/$_4$")

68

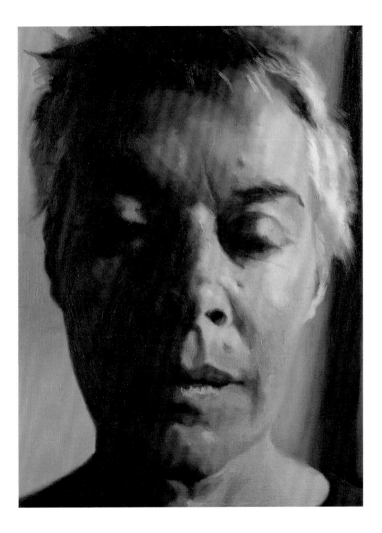

ANNIE
David Tebbs
Oil on canvas, 400 x 300mm (15³/₄ x 11⁷/₈")

69

WILLIAM PACKER
Daphne Todd
Oil on birch panels, 735 x 545mm (28$^{7}/_{8}$ x 21$^{1}/_{2}$")

70

CHRISA
Jaime Valero Perandones
Oil on board, 550 x 1005mm (21^5/$_8$ x 39^1/$_2$")

HAPPY THOUGHT – SELF-PORTRAIT
Jason Walker
Oil on canvas, 500 x 390mm (19³/₄ x 15³/₈")

KATE
Vicky White
Oil on linen on board, 605 x 400mm (23⁷/₈ x 15¹/₄")

FATHER AND SONS
Antony Williams
Egg tempera on board, 1400 x 1900mm (55¹⁄₈ x 74³⁄₄")

74

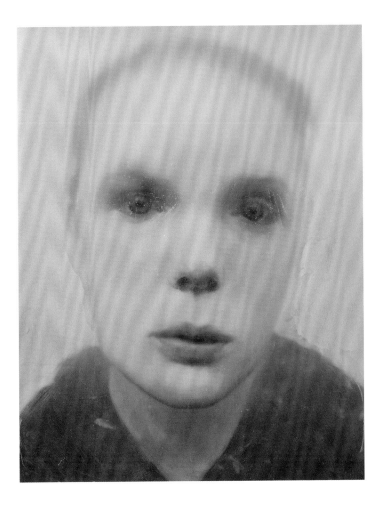

MACULAR ME
Suzy Willis
Oil and wax on canvas, 250 x 200mm (9⁷/₈ x 7⁷/₈")

75

SELF-PORTRAIT AS TWINS
Paula Wilson
Oil on board, 335 x 335mm (13^1/$_8$ x 13^1/$_8$")

CARA
Steve Wilson
Oil on board, 380 x 250mm (15 x 9⁷/₈")

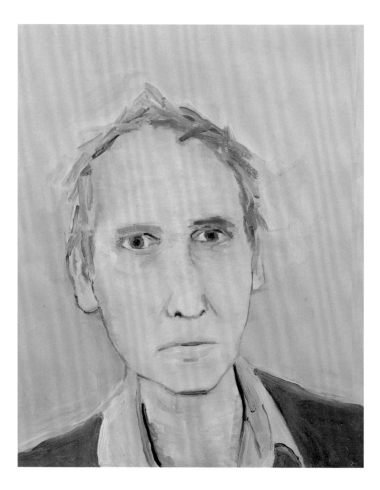

SELF-PORTRAIT
William Wright
Oil on canvas, 300 x 240mm (11$^7/_8$ x 9$^1/_2$")

BP TRAVEL AWARD INFORMATION

Each year exhibitors are invited to submit a proposal for the BP Travel Award. The aim of the Award is to give an artist the opportunity to experience working in a different environment, in Britain or abroad, on a project related to portraiture. The artist's work is then shown as part of the following year's BP Portrait Award exhibition and tour.

THE JUDGES 2006 AND 2007

Sarah Howgate, Contemporary Curator,
National Portrait Gallery

Liz Rideal, Art Education Officer,
National Portrait Gallery

Des Violaris, Director, UK Arts & Culture, BP

THE PRIZE WINNER 2006

Toby Wiggins who received £4,000 for his proposal to spend four weeks travelling around Wessex painting a farming community in crisis. Wessex is a loosely defined geographical region in south-west Britain, which spreads across rural areas of Avon, Devon, Dorset, Hampshire, Somerset and Wiltshire.

Last autumn, Toby Wiggins hired a 1972 VW camper van to travel around Wessex making portraits of people who worked the land. Here, Toby, who grew up in Dorset and spent time working on local farms, reveals how the agricultural community are coping with the rapid changes to their way of life. Toby made recordings while drawing and painting his sitters, and extracts accompany the portraits selected for this book.

TRAVELS IN A CAMPER VAN

The camper van was ideal for negotiating the narrow country lanes. After several days fighting with the gear stick, I was purring along at a top speed of 55mph.

Travelling into the New Forest, up an unmade track through mature trees, I reached the home of the verderer (whose job is to protect the New Forest's traditional landscape and its commoning practices). I was greeted by several wandering ponies, a couple of bounding dogs and Dionis MacNair, the verderer, at her porch. She took me into her kitchen, lit by tiny windows incised into deep cob walls, lined with rosettes. We sat at a table in front of a window, the side of her face lit up beautifully, her hair a striking silver. Dionis talked with authority about the New Forest she loved, practical in her analysis of its present needs and future preservation. I left with apples and pears.

From the New Forest I took in the Isle of Purbeck, moved through the Blackmore Vale and up over the Salisbury Plain, down on to the Somerset Levels and west over the Quantocks into Devon. The people I visited showed me great generosity. I often received gifts of fruit, in particular apples, field mushrooms and on occasion a roast dinner, and a glass or three of cider in Somerset. Judy Knight, a farmer, gave me some of her own Dexter beef, which I cooked up with wild mushrooms in the back of the van. Delicious!

Of the people I met, many were indigenous to the area they lived, some had migrated across Wessex and there were some newcomers. All had a strong sense of place and a passion for their work.

TOBY WIGGINS IN HIS
STUDIO IN DORSET
(OPPOSITE).

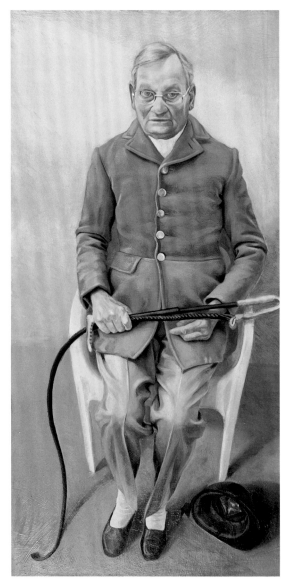

JIM BENNETT,
RETIRED HUNT SERVANT
Toby Wiggins
Oil gesso panel
760 x 380mm
(30 x 15")

'I spent my whole working life as a hunt servant. I started when I was fourteen. It was the late Lady Shaftsbury that started me into hunt service. You worked on the estate and went into the woods or you worked the land, but I just wanted to be with horses. Quite an experience for a boy to go and work in an establishment with twenty men. That's how many people worked for the Portman Hunt in those days, they hunted five or six days a week. You were working everyday from morn to night and I found it very hard. I broke a lot of bones in my time.

'The mustard coloured jacket goes back to my Berkeley days. They hunted from Berkeley Castle right up to Marble Arch years and years ago. If I had my time again, I would do the same if I could. I was brought up in a very humble way and have been very lucky.'

ROGER WILKINS
AND TOM TINKNELL,
CIDER MAKERS
Toby Wiggins
Oil on canvas
240 x 300mm
(9½ x 12")

'That's eleven layers, about thirteen hundredweight on there, and he'll run roughly ninety gallons of cider. Apple juice I'll call it now, but it will go into cider. The apple pomace [crushed apple] I'll feed to the beef cattle out in the field.'

VERDERER, NEW FOREST, HAMPSHIRE

'I've been here since 1940, a long time. The population has gone up absolutely massively. They say the houses here grow like "Topsy". The planners have been trying to cut down on allowing expansion, they haven't been very successful. We are always fighting urbanisation. Thirteen million day visitors is really rather more than can be coped with, but how can you cut it down?

'It is vital for the forest to keep commoning. They will say that they do like their animals and they hate seeing them run over ... but if you kill commoning you lose the forest, there's no doubt about it.

'The ponies have proved themselves extremely versatile as anyone can ride them, and they mostly have extremely good temperaments.

'All the roads floated on a raft of heather, mind you they still do. You would be surprised at the number of bales of heather that are under some of the main roads across the forest and the Romans did that.

'I can talk about the forest forever.'

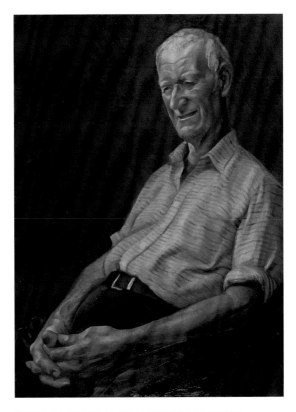

DAVID VINCENT,
PEDIGREE CATTLE
BREEDER
Toby Wiggins
Oil gesso panel
550 x 400mm
(21¾ x 15¾")

CATTLE BREEDER, WIMBOURNE, DORSET

'My father was a dairyman and I've been milking cows nearly all my life. I wouldn't like to say how many [dairy farms] have gone out of business. If it wasn't for family, they wouldn't be able to keep going. If I had to pay someone I'd have to give up, simple as that.

'I went to the Southampton docks to see an importation of German Simmental cattle; anyway I found Brown Swiss heifers. I went to the bank man and asked if I could have a loan to buy one. Now that's my show cattle besides a few British Whites. It all takes time, but that's the benefit of enjoying it and the result is a better type of cattle. It's what keeps me going.'

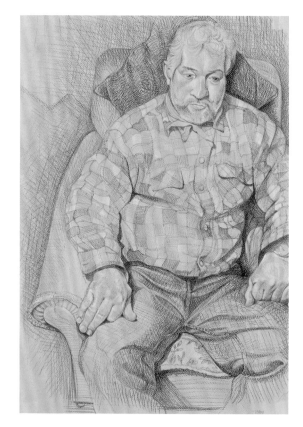

TONY COTTRELL,
THATCHER
Toby Wiggins
Pencil on paper
500 x 350mm
(19¾ x 13¾")

THATCHER, WIMBOURNE, DORSET

'This love of thatching, I just fell into it. When my dad was in the services, RAF, we lived in a thatched cottage in Wiltshire; I just loved it. My son has just qualified as a master thatcher. We practise the old style of thatching with wheat reed, spar-bonds or straw-bonds and twisted locally produced spars. Traditionally wheat reed or long straw was used in this area.

'It's a much more friendly material wheat, there's something about it – and the shape that you can create on the cottage, a nice rounded shape, a bit like custard over treacle pud.'

ACKNOWLEDGEMENTS

I should like to offer my thanks to all the artists who entered work and congratulations to those selected for exhibition, particularly the prize winners: Johan Andersson, Paul Emsley, David Lawton and Hynek Martinec. I am enormously grateful to those who gave time to serve on the jury: Jason Brooks, Rachel Campbell-Johnston, Sarah Howgate, Erin O'Connor and Des Violaris. They were immensely thoughtful in their choices. My thanks go to Lynne Truss for her essay, the galleries with which we collaborate during the exhibition tour – the Laing Art Gallery, Newcastle, and the Scottish National Portrait Gallery, Edinburgh – and the National Portrait Gallery staff who have worked hard to make the exhibition such a success, amongst them Joanna Banham, Pim Baxter, Claudia Bloch, Caroline Brooke Johnson, Denise Ellitson, Neil Evans, Ian Gardner, Tim Holton, Celia Joicey, Ruth Müller-Wirth, Liz Rideal, Jonathan Rowbotham, Jude Simmons, Sarah Tinsley, Alex Willett and especially our exhibition manager, Sue Thompson. Thanks also to the white wall company for helping during the judging process and to Anne Sørensen for designing the catalogue.

Finally I should like to offer special thanks to BP who have renewed the sponsorship of the competition and exhibition for a further five years. Such a show of confidence in the importance of the contemporary visual arts is enormously encouraging, and allows the Gallery to plan for the future with determination.

SANDY NAIRNE
Director, National Portrait Gallery

INDEX

Figures in *italics* refer to illustrations.

Ahrens, Lynn *23*
Alexander, Rupert *24*
Andersson, Johan
  (prize winner) *18*
Andrews, Jeremy *25*
Aytoun-Ellis, Maryanne *26*

Ball, John *27*
Benchley, Robert 14
Benford, Polly *28*
Bennett, Jim *82*, 83
Bitsakis, Emmanouil *29*
Brazier, Richard *30*
Brown, Vincent *31*

Cameron, Julia Margaret
  10, 11–12
Conroy, Stephen:
  Sir Jonathan Miller 9, 10
Corsham, Francis *32*
Cottrell, Tony 86, *86*

Emsley, Paul (prize winner) *19*
Escofet, Miriam *33*

Fakhr, Darvish 12, *13*, *34*
Foroozanfar, Maryam *35*

Gershuni, Aram *36*

Hall, Robin-Lee *37*
Hardy, Jaemi *38*
Helland, Ingolv *39*
Hext, Amanda *40*
Hogan, Eileen *41*
Hooper, Jill *42*
Hyman, Timothy *43*

Im, Kwang-Sik *44*

Kelley, Diarmuid *45*
Kopp, Sandro *46*

Lawton, David (prize winner) *20*
Leveritt, Thomas *47*

Macnair, Dionis 84, *84*
Madia, Anna *48*

Martinec, Hynek (prize winner) *21*
Massey, Susannah *49*
Mernini, Francesco *50*
Merton, Nicholas *51*
Micu, Ana Maria *52*
Miller, Sir Jonathan 9, 10
Morris, Luis *53*

Nelson, Neil *54*

Oxborough, Paul *55*

Penn, Morgan *56*
Pohlschmidt, Scott *57*
Pollard, Anastasia *58*

Reid, Gareth *59*
Renforth, Philip *60*
Robinson, Keith *61*
Rogers, Stephen Earl *62*

Schless, Geert *63*
Sinclair, Perdita *64*
Sullivan, Benjamin *65*
Sutcliffe, Edward *66*
Szekely, Cassandra *67*

Tafrov, Ivan *68*
Tebbs, David *69*
Terry, Ellen 11, *11*
Tinknell, Tom 83, *83*
Todd, Daphne *70*

Valero Perandones, Jaime *71*
Vincent, David 85, *85*

Walker, Jason *72*
Watts, George Frederic:
  Choosing 10–11, *11*
White, Vicky *73*
Wiggins, Toby (prize winner)
  79, 80, *81*–6
Wilkins, Roger 83, *83*
Williams, Antony *74*
Willis, Suzy *75*
Wilson, Paula *76*
Wilson, Steve *77*
Wright, William *78*